EAT YOUR GREENS!

EAT YOUR GREENS!

LEAFY GREEN RECIPES USING KALE, SPINACH AND MORE

This edition published by Parragon Books Ltd in 2014
LOVE FOOD is an imprint of Parragon Books Ltd

Parragon Books Ltd
Chartist House
15–17 Trim Street
Bath BA1 1HA, UK
www.parragon.com/lovefood

ISBN 978-1-4723-6450-0

Printed in China

New recipes, introduction and incidental text written by Christine McFadden
New photography by iangarlick.com
New food styling by Nikki Gee
Internal illustrations by Nicola O'Byrne
Project managed by Louisa Smith
Production controller: Joe Xavier

Notes for the Reader
This book uses both metric and imperial measurements. Follow the same units of measurement throughout; do not mix metric and imperial. All spoon measurements are level: teaspoons are assumed to be 5 ml, and tablespoons are assumed to be 15 ml. Unless otherwise stated, milk is assumed to be full fat, eggs and individual vegetables are medium, and pepper is freshly ground black pepper. Unless otherwise stated, all root vegetables should be peeled prior to using.

Garnishes, decorations and serving suggestions are all optional and not necessarily included in the recipe ingredients or method. The times given are an approximate guide only. Preparation times differ according to the techniques used by different people and the cooking times may also vary from those given. Optional ingredients, variations or serving suggestions have not been included in the time calculations.

Picture acknowledgements
The publisher would like to thank the following for the permission to reproduce copyright material: page 7 (radicchio) © Fuse/Getty Images; page 117 (tray of sodas in bottles) © Cultura/BRETT STEVENS/Getty Images.

CONTENTS

INTRODUCTION

Not so long ago, the thought of cooking and eating green vegetables was likely to produce a sigh rather than a smile. How things have changed! Thanks to an ever-increasing choice of gorgeous greens in the shops and imaginative new ideas for ways of cooking them, not to mention the growing evidence pointing to their nutritional credentials, we are finally eating our greens. These once unloved vegetables are now the food heroes of the century and a green force to be reckoned with.

So what's so great about greens? Why do we need to eat them? First of all, as the recipes in this book prove, they taste fantastic. What's more, they're a breeze to cook and they're incredibly versatile – you can eat them raw or roasted, steamed or stir-fried, tossed into salads, made into a juice, packed into pancakes or stirred into stews. Depending on what you serve them with, greens are as easy on the purse as they are on the waistline. But probably most importantly, they're packed with must-have nutrients that make you feel good. What's not to like?

KNOW YOUR GREENS

GREENS FOR COOKING
Kale

Impeccable nutritional credentials and stylish good looks have made kale a culinary super-star. Depending on variety, the leaves are either flamboyantly frilled or deeply serrated. Some are a luminous blue-green contrasting with beautiful purple stalks; while others are so dark they could almost be black. The flavour is satisfyingly rich and earthy, with a pleasant hint of sweetness. Kale is wonderfully versatile: steam, boil, sauté; braise with a grain; simmer in soups and stews; whizz into pesto for pasta; or add young leaves to salads. For a moreish nibble, toss torn leaves with oil and roast in a low oven until crisp.

Spinach

There are two basic types of spinach: smooth-leaved, stalk-free baby spinach for eating raw, and the larger puckered leaves (with stalks) that are better cooked. Both have a melt-in-the-mouth texture, and an earthy, almost salty flavour. Spinach can be boiled, steamed, stir-fried or wilted in butter or oil. It blends happily with other ingredients – use it in pasta dishes, risotto and as a pizza topping. Bear in mind that the leaves reduce by at least half once cooked.

Chard

With chard you get two vegetables for the price of one – crunchy stalks and melt-in-the-mouth leaves. The stalks, which take longer to cook, make a tasty side dish and are also good in a gratin or stir-fry. The leaves are used in the same way as spinach. Some varieties have spectacular technicolour stalks and crinkly dark-green leaves. Swiss chard has broad white stalks and smooth grass-green leaves. The flavour is rich and earthy, similar to spinach but punchier.

Cabbage

Cabbages range from dense drumhead types and crinkly Savoys to looser-leaved, conical spring cabbages and crisp Chinese cabbage. They come in a palette of colours: creamy pale yellow, luminous shades of green and rich ruby-red. Often under-appreciated, cabbage is delicious lightly cooked, slowly braised, or shredded and served raw in a salad. The flavour ranges from mild and sweet spring cabbage and peppery red cabbage to the more challenging meatiness of the dense green varieties. For a side dish, steaming is preferable to boiling. Stir-frying and braising are good if you are after something more substantial. Fresh herbs lift the flavour, as does grated lemon rind and plenty of freshly ground black pepper.

Roasted Broccoli with Pine Nuts & Parmesan (page 82)

Brussels sprouts

Brussels sprouts look like walnut-sized cabbages. They are usually sold loose, but you can sometimes find them still attached to a long, rigid stem. Most are bright-green in colour, although ruby-red varieties also exist. Sprouts have a dense texture and a satisfyingly meaty, slightly sweet flavour. They are delicious lightly steamed, boiled or stir-fried. Halve or quarter them if large, and cook until just tender – overcooked sprouts will disintegrate and smell unpleasant. Shredded finely, sprouts are surprisingly delicious eaten raw in coleslaw or a winter salad.

Broccoli

Calabrese-type broccoli has a thick central stalk and a single head of tightly packed florets of tiny unopened flower buds. Sprouting broccoli has long, slender stalks, with offshoots of thinner stalks and leaves, and small purple or cream sprouting flower heads. Both have a meaty, full-bodied flavour. If not overcooked, calabrese has a crunchy texture, whereas sprouting broccoli is softer and chewier. Both types of broccoli are best steamed, stir-fried or roasted rather than boiled – the texture is better and fewer nutrients are lost in the cooking water. Serve as a side dish or add small florets and sliced stalks to risotto, pasta dishes and thick tortilla-style omelettes. Sprouting broccoli is delicious cooked like asparagus – steamed or grilled – and anointed with olive oil or melted butter.

Tuna with Pak Choi & Soba Noodles (page 74)

Pak choi

One of the most delicious Asian greens, pak choi (also called bok choy) has edible ivory-white stalks and broad green leaves. Some varieties have thicker spoon-shaped stalks, and some have ruby-red leaves. The stalks are crisp and juicy with a hint of sweetness, while the leaves have a slight mustard tang. Pak choi is delicious both raw and cooked. Slice and add to salads, or use in stir-fries, soups and noodle dishes. The stalks take slightly longer to cook than the leaves.

Collard greens

Collard greens are an ancient type of leafy green, similar to kale and spring greens. The paddle-shaped leaves are green or blue-green with a fibrous stalk. They need lengthy cooking to soften them, although shredding will speed things up. Their flavour is intensely cabbage-like with just a hint of bitterness. One of the most nutritionally rich vegetables, collard greens are good boiled, braised or stir-fried, added to soups and stews, or stuffed and rolled like cabbage leaves. Discard the stalk if it is very tough.

Mustard greens

Mustard greens are bracingly pungent – chew on some and you'll find your sinuses clear instantly. The leaves are striking – some are tinted purple-red with acid-green stalks, while others are completely green. Added sparingly, small young leaves add pep and colour to a salad. Larger ones are best tamed by stir-frying. Asian seasonings, such as ginger, garlic and chilli, are good companions.

Turnip greens

Turnip greens come from varieties of turnip grown for their leaves rather than for their roots. They have thick stalks and a strong peppery flavour similar to that of mustard greens. Discard the stalks, then slice the leaves into broad ribbons before cooking. Steam or boil until tender, or gently fry them in butter or olive oil. Serve as a side dish, or add to soups and stews.

SALAD GREENS

Lettuce

Top of the lettuce league for crunch and full-bodied flavour is romaine – essential for the classic Caesar salad. High in crunch but low in flavour is iceberg – the bowl-shaped leaves make a crisp wrapping for a tasty filling and they are good shredded and served in a roll with burgers. Loose-headed butterhead has large soft leaves with a lovely sweet flavour – perfect for a simple green salad. Smaller with a tightly packed heart, Little Gem is also excellent for green salads. Bronze-tinged red oak and frilly lollo rosso add contrasting texture and colour. Lettuce can also be used to make a vibrant soup or juice, or try it lightly braised with peas and new potatoes.

Endive

Often confused with chicories, endives include frisée (curly endive) and escarole (Batavia). Frisée has deeply serrated, slightly coarse leaves, while escarole leaves are smoother at the edges and softer. Both have dark-green outer leaves and lemon-yellow hearts. The flavour is sweet with just a hint of bitterness. Mixed with other leaves, endives add crisp texture to a salad and are an excellent foil to rich meat dishes.

Rocket

Rocket has a distinctive peppery flavour and pleasantly chewy texture. Wild rocket has small, deeply notched, dark-green leaves, while the more common variety has longer leaves with shallower notches. Essential for Mediterranean-style salads, rocket can also be steamed or gently fried in oil and tossed with pasta.

Watercress

A feisty member of the Brassica family, watercress has a complex, peppery flavour. It is at its best served simply in a salad, perhaps with red onion slivers or shaved fennel, and it makes an excellent sandwich filling. Lightly wilted watercress is delicious tossed with pasta, or stirred into an omelette or a risotto. It also makes a vibrant green soup.

Radicchio

A round-headed chicory variety, radicchio has tightly furled burgundy-red leaves with white stalks and veins. The slightly chewy leaves have a bittersweet flavour. They are best sliced and added sparingly to a salad. Radicchio is also very good brushed with oil and grilled, or braised and added to risotto or pasta.

LIGHT BITES

RADICCHIO CAESAR SALAD

The classic Caesar salad is made with romaine lettuce, but here ruby-red radicchio is used instead. Its bittersweet flavour goes well with the Parmesan, pancetta and mustard dressing.

SERVES: 2   **PREP TIME: 20 MINS**   **COOK TIME: 5 MINS**

INGREDIENTS

4 thin slices pancetta

½ head of radicchio, tough outer leaves and coarse stems removed

55 g/2 oz ready-made croûtons

4 anchovies in oil, drained (optional)

25 g/1 oz freshly grated Parmesan cheese, plus extra shavings to garnish

fresh basil leaves, to garnish

DRESSING

2 tsp lemon juice

1 tsp Dijon mustard

1 small garlic clove, crushed

dash of Worcestershire sauce

3 tbsp extra virgin olive oil

salt and pepper

1. To make the dressing, combine the lemon juice, mustard, garlic and Worcestershire sauce in a small bowl. Add salt and pepper to taste, then gradually whisk in the oil until thick.

2. Add the pancetta to a dry frying pan and fry for 2–3 minutes, until crisp. Drain on kitchen paper. Break into bite-sized pieces and set aside.

3. Tear the radicchio leaves into bite-sized pieces. Place in a salad bowl with the croûtons, anchovies (if using), and the grated Parmesan. Whisk the dressing, pour over the leaves and toss to coat.

4. Top the salad with the reserved pancetta, the Parmesan shavings and basil leaves. Serve immediately.

PURPLE SPROUTING BROCCOLI SALAD

SERVES: 4   **PREP TIME: 15 MINS**   **COOK TIME: 15 MINS**

INGREDIENTS

200 g/7 oz purple sprouting broccoli

250 g/9 oz red cabbage, shredded

115 g/4 oz cooked beetroot in natural juices (drained weight), drained and cut into matchsticks

2 tbsp dried cranberries

3 tbsp balsamic vinegar

CROÛTONS

2 tbsp olive oil

85 g/3 oz rustic wholegrain bread, torn into small pieces

1 tbsp sunflower seeds

1 tbsp flaxseeds (linseeds)

1. Put the broccoli in the top of a steamer, cover and set over a saucepan of simmering water. Steam for 3–5 minutes, or until tender. Cool under cold running water, then cut the stems in half and the lower stems in half again lengthways, and transfer them to a salad bowl.

2. Add the red cabbage, beetroot and dried cranberries to the salad bowl.

3. To make the croûtons, heat the oil in a frying pan over a medium heat, add the bread and fry for 3–4 minutes, stirring, until just beginning to brown. Add the sunflower seeds and flaxseeds and cook for a further 2–3 minutes, until lightly toasted.

4. Drizzle the balsamic vinegar over the salad and toss gently together. Sprinkle with the croûtons and serve immediately.

HERO TIPS

The darker the broccoli florets – either purple, green or deep blue-green – the higher the amounts of beta-carotene and vitamin C they contain.

SMOKED SALMON & PINK GRAPEFRUIT SALAD

SERVES: 2   **PREP TIME: 20 MINS**   **COOK TIME: NONE**

INGREDIENTS

1 pink grapefruit
50 g/1¾ oz rocket
50 g/1¾ oz frisée
½ fennel bulb, thinly sliced
large pinch of sea salt
1 tbsp extra virgin olive oil, plus extra for drizzling
½ tsp white wine vinegar
60 g/2¼ oz smoked salmon
pepper
salad cress, to garnish

1. Using a sharp knife, cut a slice from the top and bottom of the grapefruit. Remove the peel and white pith by cutting downwards, following the shape of the fruit as closely as possible. Cut between the flesh and membrane of each segment and ease out the flesh. Discard the membrane and set aside the flesh.

2. Put the rocket, frisée and fennel in a bowl. Sprinkle with the sea salt. Gently toss with your hands to distribute the salt. Add the oil and gently toss. Sprinkle with the vinegar, toss again and divide between two serving plates.

3. Cut the smoked salmon into bite-sized pieces and arrange on top of the salad with the grapefruit segments. Drizzle with oil and sprinkle with pepper.

4. Garnish with salad cress and serve immediately.

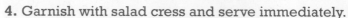

SEARED BEEF SALAD

A Thai-inspired salad with thinly sliced steak served over nutrient-boosting kale, sliced peppery radishes and cool mint and coriander, all drizzled with a zesty lime dressing.

SERVES: 4 **PREP TIME: 15 MINS** **COOK TIME: 10 MINS**

INGREDIENTS

½ iceberg lettuce, leaves separated and torn into bite-sized pieces

200 g/7 oz radishes, thinly sliced

4 shallots, thinly sliced

85 g/3 oz kale, shredded

2 tbsp dried goji berries

25 g/1 oz fresh mint, roughly chopped

25 g/1 oz fresh coriander, roughly chopped

2 sirloin steaks, about 250 g/9 oz each, visible fat removed

1 tbsp sunflower oil

salt and pepper

DRESSING

juice of 1 lime

1 tbsp soy sauce

3 tbsp sunflower oil

1. Put the lettuce, radishes and shallots in a serving bowl. Sprinkle over the kale, goji berries, mint and coriander, then toss gently.

2. Preheat a ridged griddle pan over a high heat. Brush the steaks with the oil, then sprinkle with a little salt and pepper. Cook in the hot pan for 2 minutes on each side for medium-rare, 3 minutes for medium or 4 minutes for well done. Transfer the steaks to a plate and leave to rest for a few minutes.

3. Meanwhile, to make the dressing, put the lime juice, soy sauce and oil in a clean jam jar, screw on the lid and shake well. Drizzle over the salad, then toss together.

4. Divide the salad between four bowls. Thinly slice the steak and arrange it over the top, then serve immediately.

GADO GADO SALAD

In this Indonesian-inspired salad, raw broccoli and cabbage are tossed with crunchy beansprouts and cucumber and coated with a delicious peanut and soy dressing.

SERVES: 4   **PREP TIME: 20 MINS**   **COOK TIME: 5 MINS PLUS COOLING**

INGREDIENTS

250 g/9 oz cauliflower, cut into small florets

115 g/4 oz broccoli, cut into small florets

115 g/4 oz Savoy cabbage, shredded

150 g/5½ oz fresh beansprouts

300 g/10½ oz cucumber, peeled, halved lengthways, deseeded and thickly sliced

1 red pepper, deseeded and finely chopped

DRESSING

2 tbsp groundnut oil

85 g/3 oz unsalted peanuts, finely chopped

2 garlic cloves, finely chopped

2 tbsp soy sauce

juice of 2 limes

½ red chilli, deseeded and finely chopped

1. Put the cauliflower, broccoli, cabbage, beansprouts, cucumber and red pepper in a salad bowl and toss gently.

2. To make the dressing, heat 1 tablespoon of the oil in a frying pan over a medium heat. Add the peanuts and garlic and stir-fry for 2–3 minutes, or until lightly browned. Remove from the heat and stir in the soy sauce, lime juice, chilli and the remaining oil, then leave to cool.

3. Spoon the dressing over the salad and toss gently. Divide between four bowls and serve immediately.

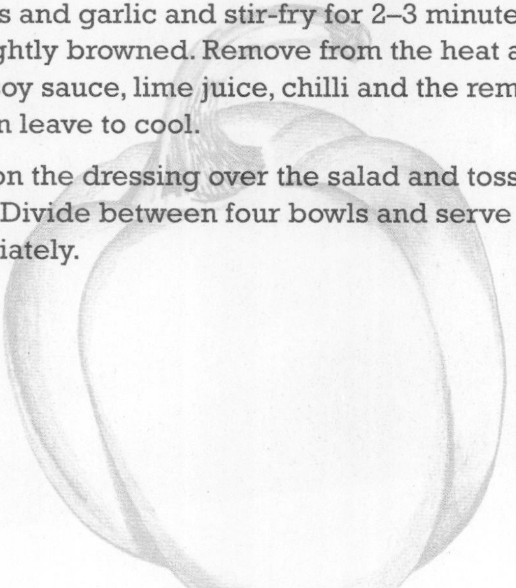

GREEN CREDENTIALS

Green vegetables boast an extraordinary range of health-promoting nutrients. Not only do they provide vitamins, minerals and fibre, they're also packed with phytochemicals – a group of substances that make up a kind of anti-carcinogenic cocktail that stimulates the body's defences.

Among the most important substances are antioxidants. These include several minerals, vitamins C and E, and carotenoids (the plant version of vitamin A). Antioxidants protect the body by deactivating harmful free radicals that attack the nucleus of body cells, causing genetic changes that have been linked to cancer.

And that's not all. Green vegetables contain folate, a type of B vitamin needed for healthy red blood cells and especially important for growing children and pregnant women. They provide essential minerals, too, particularly those needed by women: calcium to help prevent osteoporosis (loss of bone mass) later in life, and iron to replace that lost in blood during menstruation. Just a few good reasons to eat your greens!

NUTRIENTS AND WHAT THEY DO:

Calcium

Strengthens the bones. Essential for muscle contraction, nerve function, enzyme activity and blood clotting.

Iron

Involved in red blood cell production and transporting oxygen around the body.

Folate

A type of B vitamin vital for forming new cells and therefore essential for growing embryos. Also needed for normal development in children.

Vitamin A/Carotenoids

Vitamin A is found in food from animal sources but it is also made from carotenoids in plant foods that convert to vitamin A in the body. Carotenoids are a group of substances that protect the cells, boost the immune system and protect the skin from sun damage.

Vitamin C

Helps the body absorb iron from food. Also speeds up wound healing, helps keep skin supple and boosts resistance to infection.

Important nutrients in greens (per 100 g/3½ oz, raw)

	Calcium mg	Iron mg	Folate µg	Vitamin A iu	Vitamin C mg
Broccoli	47	0.73	63	623	89.2 (2nd)
Brussels sprouts	42	1.4	61	754	85 (3rd)
Lettuce, green leaf	36	0.86	38	2,666	9.2
Chard	51	1.8 (2nd)	14	6,116	30
Collard greens	232 (1st)	0.47	129	5,019	35.3
Endives	52	0.83	142 (2nd)	2,167	6.5
Kale	150 (3rd)	1.47	141 (3rd)	9,990 (2nd)	120 (1st)
Watercress	120	0.20	9	3,191	43
Mustard greens	115	1.64 (3rd)	12	3,024	70
Cabbage	40	0.47	43	98	36.6
Spinach	99	2.71 (1st)	194 (1st)	9,377 (3rd)	28.1
Turnip greens	190 (2nd)	1.10	194 (1st)	11,587 (1st)	60
Pak choi	105	0.8	66	4,468	45

Sources: USDA database

 Vegetable containing the most of a particular nutrient

 Runners-up for each nutrient

PORK & COCONUT LETTUCE WRAPS

Crisp bowl-shaped leaves of iceberg or Webbs lettuce make a crunchy wrap for this spicy filling. Fold the leaves around the meat and eat with your fingers.

SERVES: 4   **PREP TIME: 15 MINS**   **COOK TIME: 10 MINS**

INGREDIENTS

40 g/1½ oz dried coconut chips

1 tsp fennel seeds

1 tsp cumin seeds

3 tbsp coconut oil or vegetable oil

2 shallots, chopped

1 garlic clove, thinly sliced

¼–½ tsp dried red chilli flakes

225 g/8 oz fresh pork mince

juice of ½ lime

6 tbsp chopped fresh coriander

8 large, crisp lettuce leaves, such as iceberg or Webbs, thick stems removed

salt and pepper

finely sliced fresh red chilli, to garnish

soy sauce and lime wedges, to serve

1. Preheat the oven to 180°C/350°F/Gas Mark 4.

2. Spread the coconut chips on a baking tray. Toast in the preheated oven for 2–3 minutes, until beginning to turn golden. Remove from the oven and set aside.

3. Place the fennel seeds and cumin seeds in a mortar and lightly crush with a pestle. Heat the oil in a frying pan over a medium–high heat. Add the shallots, garlic, crushed fennel and cumin seeds and chilli flakes and fry for 2 minutes, until just coloured.

4. Stir in all but 4 tablespoons of the coconut chips. Add the pork, breaking up any clumps with a fork, and fry for 3 minutes, until no longer pink. Stir in the lime juice and 4 tablespoons of the coriander. Season to taste with salt and pepper.

5. Divide the pork mixture between the lettuce leaves and arrange on a serving platter. Sprinkle with the remaining coconut chips and coriander. Garnish with chilli slices and serve immediately with a bowl of soy sauce for dipping and lime wedges for squeezing over.

TURKEY WRAPS WITH AVOCADO SALSA

SERVES: 4

PREP TIME: 30 MINS PLUS MARINATING

COOK TIME: 10 MINS

INGREDIENTS

4 thin turkey breast escalopes, 350 g/12 oz total weight

olive oil, for brushing

4 romaine or cos lettuce leaves, thick stems removed, leaves sliced into ribbons

4 corn tortillas, warmed

3 tbsp soured cream

MARINADE

juice of 2 oranges

1 tsp cumin seeds, lightly crushed

½ tsp dried red chilli flakes

4 tbsp olive oil

salt and pepper

SALSA

2 avocados, peeled, stoned and diced

1 small red onion, diced

2 tomatoes, deseeded and diced

2 tbsp chopped fresh coriander

juice of 1 lime

1. Slice the turkey into 4 x 6-cm/1½ x 2½-inch strips. Place in a shallow dish.

2. To make the marinade, whisk together all the marinade ingredients. Pour over the turkey, cover and marinate in the refrigerator for 4 hours, or overnight. Remove from the refrigerator at least 30 minutes before cooking to bring to room temperature.

3. To make the salsa, combine all the ingredients in a small bowl.

4. Preheat the grill to very high. Drain the turkey, discarding the marinade. Thread the strips concertina-style onto metal skewers (or use wooden skewers with aluminium foil wrapped around the ends so that they don't burn) and brush with oil. Place the skewers on a rack in the grill pan and cook under the preheated grill for about 5 minutes on each side, until the turkey is cooked through and starting to brown at the edges. Remove the turkey from the skewers, set aside and keep warm.

5. Divide the lettuce between the tortillas and arrange the turkey on top. Add a little soured cream and salsa. Roll the bottoms and sides of the tortillas over the filling and serve immediately.

ROCKET, WHITE BEAN & TOMATO BRUSCHETTA

In this dish, crisp toasted sourdough is topped with peppery rocket, tomato slivers and a moreish mix of crushed beans, garlic and herbs. It's easy to make and hard to beat as a snack or starter.

SERVES: 4   **PREP TIME: 20 MINS**   **COOK TIME: 5 MINS**

INGREDIENTS

800 g/1 lb 12 oz canned cannellini beans, drained and rinsed

1 garlic clove, crushed

2 tbsp extra virgin olive oil, plus extra for drizzling

1 tsp lemon juice

1 tbsp chopped fresh flat-leaf parsley

¾ tsp chopped fresh rosemary leaves

25 g/1 oz rocket

8–10 slices sourdough bread

16–20 baby plum tomatoes, quartered lengthways

sea salt and pepper

1. Combine the beans, garlic, oil, lemon juice, parsley and rosemary in a large bowl. Season to taste with sea salt and pepper, then mash to a chunky purée with a fork.

2. Roughly chop the rocket leaves if they are very large. Preheat the grill to medium.

3. Place the bread under the preheated grill and toast on both sides.

4. Thickly spread the bread with the bean purée. Pile the rocket on top, followed by the tomato quarters. Sprinkle with sea salt and pepper, drizzle with a little oil and serve immediately.

BUCKWHEAT PANCAKES WITH SPINACH & FETA

MAKES: 8

PREP TIME: 30 MINS PLUS RESTING

COOK TIME: 45 MINS

INGREDIENTS

60 g/2¼ oz buckwheat flour

40 g/1½ oz plain flour

2 eggs, lightly beaten

350 ml/12 fl oz milk

25 g/1 oz butter, plus extra for frying

125 g/4½ oz chestnut mushrooms, halved or thickly sliced

600 g/1 lb 5 oz baby spinach

35 g/1¼ oz walnuts, roughly chopped

50 g/1¾ oz feta cheese, crumbled

large pinch of freshly grated nutmeg

large pinch of dried red chilli flakes

salt and pepper

snipped fresh chives, to garnish

1. Sift together the buckwheat flour, plain flour and ½ teaspoon salt into a large bowl. Make a well in the centre and drop in the eggs. Using a fork, mix in some of the flour from the edge of the bowl. Gradually add the milk, stirring to a smooth batter. Set aside for 30 minutes, then melt the 25 g/1 oz butter in a small saucepan and whisk into the batter.

2. Melt a knob of butter in a large frying pan, add the mushrooms and fry for 5 minutes. Remove from the heat and set aside.

3. Meanwhile, steam the spinach for 4 minutes. Drain, squeezing out as much liquid as possible, then roughly chop. Add the walnuts and feta to the mushrooms and mix well. Add the spinach, nutmeg, chilli flakes, and salt and pepper to taste. Keep warm over a very low heat.

4. Add a knob of butter to a 24-cm/9½-inch non-stick frying pan and place over a medium heat until sizzling. Pour in 4 tablespoons of the batter, rotating the pan to distribute evenly. Fry for 2–2½ minutes on each side, turning carefully, until flecked with brown. Set aside and keep warm while you cook seven more pancakes in the same way.

5. Spoon some of the filling down the middle of each pancake. Roll up, then slice in half. Garnish with chives and serve immediately.

STEAK SANDWICHES WITH CARAMELIZED ONIONS

SERVES: 4   **PREP TIME: 15 MINS**   **COOK TIME: 50 MINS**

INGREDIENTS

2 sirloin steaks, about
225 g/8 oz each

2 red onions, sliced into
thick rings

3 tbsp olive oil, plus extra for
brushing and drizzling

2 tsp sugar

2 tsp balsamic vinegar

8 slices sourdough bread

1 beef tomato, sliced

50 g/1¾ oz rocket

salt and pepper

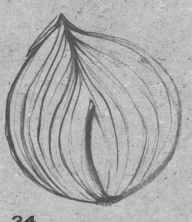

1. Preheat the oven to 190°C/375°F/Gas Mark 5.

2. Lightly brush the steaks with oil, sprinkle with salt and pepper and set aside at room temperature.

3. Put the onion rings in a large bowl with the 3 tablespoons oil, the sugar, and salt and pepper to taste. Toss well, separating the rings. Spread out in a roasting tin. Roast in the preheated oven for 20–25 minutes, stirring every 10 minutes, until just beginning to brown. Sprinkle with the vinegar, stir and spread out. Roast for a further 5–8 minutes, until brown and sticky. Tip into a bowl and set aside.

4. Heat a ridged griddle pan over a medium–high heat. Add the steaks and fry for 3–3½ minutes on each side. Transfer to a board and leave to rest for 5 minutes. Preheat the grill to medium.

5. Place the bread under the preheated grill and toast on both sides. Arrange the tomato slices and rocket on four of the toast slices. Drizzle with a little oil and sprinkle with salt and pepper.

6. Carve each steak diagonally into 2-cm/¾-inch slices. Arrange on top of the rocket, then add a few caramelized onion rings (store any leftover onions in an airtight container in the refrigerator for up to one month). Top with the remaining toast slices and serve immediately.

GET FRESH!

Nowadays we have a good choice of places to buy green vegetables, from supermarkets and greengrocers to farmer's markets, farm shops and vegetable box schemes, to name a few. Supermarkets probably provide the widest choice, usually with year-round availability. Much of the produce is pre-packaged, pre-washed and pre-prepared – a great convenience if you lead an action-packed life.

How long will my greens last?

Regardless of whether you buy greens pre-packaged or loose, there is no knowing how long they will last once you get them home. Pre-packaged greens will usually be marked with a 'display until' date, but even that doesn't necessarily mean they will stay fresh until then. So it makes sense to understand what to look for in terms of freshness, and, equally important, to know how to store your greens once you get them back home.

What's the best way of storing greens?

Keep all your greens in the refrigerator salad drawer in a brown paper bag, or a ventilated plastic bag. This provides the slightly humid but well-ventilated atmosphere that they need. A sealed plastic bag is better for watercress and fragile leafy greens that need an enclosed moist environment.

How do I know they are fresh?

In general, greens should be full of crispness and bounce, particularly the leafy types.

Broccoli

Look for bright-green heads. Avoid any that are flabby, yellowing or cracked at the cut end of the stalk. Choose sprouting broccoli with undamaged florets.

Brussels sprouts

Look for firm, tightly packed buds. Don't buy them if the outer leaves are yellow or limp.

Cabbage

Choose heads that feel heavy with crisp leaves. Reject any with yellowing outer leaves, or if the outer leaves have been stripped.

Chard, collard greens, kale and pak choi

Look for crisp, fresh leaves and firm stalks. Don't buy if the leaves are limp or yellowing, or the stalks are bruised.

Spinach and turnip tops

Look for dewy-fresh, dark-green leaves. Give them a miss if bruised, yellowing or slimy.

Lettuce, endive and mustard greens

Look for dewy-fresh leaves and firm centres for hearting lettuces. Don't buy any with brown or slimy leaves.

Radicchio

Look for tightly packed, firm heads. Don't buy them if the outer leaves have been removed.

Rocket and watercress

Look for sprightly, bright-green leaves. Give them a miss if yellowing or slimy.

KALE & POTATO CAKES WITH FRIED EGGS

SERVES: 4   **PREP TIME: 30 MINS**   **COOK TIME: 35 MINS**

INGREDIENTS

450 g/1 lb potatoes, unpeeled, cut into large chunks

100 g/3½ oz kale, thick stems removed

large knob of butter

4 spring onions, some green included, finely chopped

2 tsp dill seeds

1 tsp finely grated lemon rind

5 tbsp vegetable oil

4 eggs

salt and pepper

1. Put the potatoes in a large saucepan of lightly salted water. Bring to the boil and cook for 15–20 minutes, until tender but not disintegrating.

2. Meanwhile, bring a separate saucepan of water to the boil. Add the kale and blanch for 2 minutes. Drain and rinse under cold running water, squeezing out as much liquid as possible. Chop roughly.

3. Drain the potatoes, then return them to the pan for a few minutes to dry. Mash with the butter and salt and pepper to taste.

4. Combine the potatoes, kale, spring onions, dill seeds and lemon rind in a large bowl, mixing well with a fork. Season to taste with salt and pepper and shape into four 1 cm/½ inch thick patties.

5. Heat 3 tablespoons of the oil in a large, non-stick frying pan over a medium heat. Add the patties and fry for 3–3½ minutes on each side, turning carefully, until golden. Set aside and keep warm.

6. Heat the remaining oil in the pan, break in the eggs and fry until cooked to your liking. Place a fried egg on top of each patty. Serve immediately.

3

4

6

SPINACH & PINE NUT FRITTATA

SERVES: 4   **PREP TIME: 20 MINS**   **COOK TIME: 20 MINS**

INGREDIENTS

250 g/9 oz baby spinach
1 tbsp vegetable oil
25 g/1 oz butter
1 large shallot, halved lengthways and finely sliced
1 garlic clove, thinly sliced
40 g/1½ oz toasted pine nuts
¼ tsp dried red chilli flakes
8 eggs
25 g/1 oz freshly grated Parmesan cheese
salt and pepper
leafy green salad, to serve

1. Wash the spinach thoroughly. Drain and put into a saucepan without any extra water. Cover and cook over a medium heat for 5 minutes, stirring occasionally, until just tender. Drain, squeezing out as much liquid as possible, then roughly chop.

2. Heat the oil and butter in a 24-cm/9½-inch non-stick frying pan over a medium heat. Add the shallot and fry for 3 minutes, until translucent. Add the garlic and fry for a further 2 minutes. Stir in the spinach, pine nuts and chilli flakes. Season to taste with salt and pepper.

3. Beat the eggs in a large jug with the Parmesan. Pour into the pan, stirring to distribute the spinach evenly. Cover and cook over a medium–low heat for 5–7 minutes, until almost set. Meanwhile, preheat the grill to medium.

4. Place the pan under the preheated grill for 1–2 minutes to finish cooking the top of the frittata. Slice into wedges and serve with a leafy green salad.

HERO TIPS

It's important to use a 24-cm/9½-inch pan. If the pan is bigger, the egg mixture won't be deep enough to submerge the vegetables.

LENTIL & CHARD SOUP

SERVES: 6   **PREP TIME:** 20 MINS   **COOK TIME:** 55 MINS

INGREDIENTS

150 g/5½ oz brown lentils

1 onion, finely diced

400 ml/14 fl oz passata

600–750 ml/1–1¼ pints chicken stock or vegetable stock

½ tsp cumin seeds, lightly crushed, plus extra to garnish

350 g/12 oz chard

175 g/6 oz potatoes, cut into 1-cm/½-inch cubes

6 tbsp chopped fresh mint

2 wholemeal pittas

6 tbsp Greek-style yogurt

salt and pepper

lemon wedges, to garnish

1. Put the lentils in a large saucepan with the onion, passata, 600 ml/1 pint of the stock, the ½ teaspoon cumin seeds and ½ teaspoon salt. Bring to the boil, then cover and simmer over a low heat for 20 minutes, until the lentils are just tender.

2. Remove the stems from the chard and thinly slice. Slice the leaves crossways into ribbons.

3. Add the chard stems and potatoes to the lentils and cook for 10 minutes.

4. Add the chard leaves and cook for a further 15 minutes. If necessary, add the remaining stock to thin the soup – but it should still be quite thick. Stir in 4 tablespoons of the mint and season to taste with salt and pepper.

5. Meanwhile, preheat the grill to medium. Open out the pittas and toast under the preheated grill for 3 minutes, until crisp. Break into bite-sized pieces and arrange around the edge of six soup plates.

6. Ladle the soup into the plates. Add 1 tablespoon of yogurt to each and sprinkle with the remaining mint and cumin seeds. Garnish with lemon wedges and serve immediately.

LEEK, POTATO & SPINACH SOUP

SERVES: 4 **PREP TIME: 15 MINS** **COOK TIME: 40 MINS**

INGREDIENTS

25 g/1 oz butter

2 leeks, halved lengthways and thinly sliced

225 g/8 oz potatoes, cut into bite-sized chunks

300 g/10½ oz spinach, stalks discarded, leaves sliced

300 ml/10 fl oz vegetable stock

1 tsp lemon juice

pinch of freshly grated nutmeg

salt and pepper

soured cream, to serve

1. Melt the butter in a large saucepan over a low–medium heat. Add the leeks and potatoes, cover and cook gently for 10 minutes, or until beginning to soften.

2. Stir in 200 g/7 oz of the spinach. Cover and cook for 2–3 minutes, until starting to wilt. Season to taste with salt and pepper. Stir in half the stock. Bring to the boil, then simmer, partially covered, for 20 minutes.

3. Transfer half the soup to a food processor and process until smooth. Return to the pan.

4. Purée the remaining uncooked spinach and stock. Add to the soup in the pan. Stir in the lemon juice and nutmeg and gently reheat.

5. Ladle into bowls, swirl in a spoonful of soured cream and serve immediately.

HERO TIPS

If you'd prefer a smooth soup, transfer all the soup to the food processor in step 3 and process until smooth. You may need to do this in batches.

LETTUCE & ROCKET SOUP

SERVES: 6   **PREP TIME: 20 MINS**   **COOK TIME: 55 MINS**

INGREDIENTS

15 g/½ oz butter

1 large onion, halved and sliced

2 leeks, sliced

1.5 litres/2½ pints vegetable stock

85 g/3 oz white rice

2 carrots, sliced

3 garlic cloves, peeled

1 bay leaf

2 heads of soft, round lettuce (about 450 g/1 lb), cored and roughly chopped

175 ml/6 fl oz double cream

freshly grated nutmeg, to taste

85 g/3 oz rocket, roughly chopped, plus extra leaves to garnish

salt and pepper

1. Melt the butter in a large saucepan over a medium heat and add the onion and leeks. Cover and cook, stirring frequently, for 3–4 minutes, until the vegetables begin to soften.

2. Add the stock, rice, carrots, garlic and bay leaf with a large pinch of salt. Bring just to the boil, then reduce the heat, cover and simmer for 25–30 minutes, or until the rice and vegetables are tender. Remove and discard the bay leaf.

3. Add the lettuce to the saucepan and cook, stirring occasionally, for 10 minutes, until the leaves are wilted.

4. Remove the saucepan from the heat and leave to cool slightly. Transfer to a food processor or blender, in batches if necessary, and process until smooth.

5. Return the soup to the rinsed-out pan and reheat gently; do not boil. Stir in the cream and add nutmeg to taste. Simmer, stirring occasionally, for 5 minutes, until warmed through.

6. Add the rocket and simmer, stirring occasionally, for 2–3 minutes, until wilted. Taste and adjust the seasoning, adding salt and pepper if needed. Ladle the soup into warmed bowls, top each serving with a few rocket leaves and serve immediately.

MIGHTY MAINS

KALE, LEMON & CHIVE LINGUINE

SERVES: 2-3   **PREP TIME: 20 MINS**   **COOK TIME: 20 MINS**

INGREDIENTS

250 g/9 oz kale, thick stems removed, leaves sliced crossways into thin ribbons

225 g/8 oz dried linguine

8 tbsp olive oil

1 onion, chopped

1 garlic clove, very thinly sliced

grated rind of 1 large lemon

large pinch of dried red chilli flakes

3 tbsp snipped fresh chives

4 tbsp freshly grated Parmesan cheese

salt and pepper

1. Bring a large saucepan of water to the boil. Add the kale and blanch for 2 minutes, until just wilted. Drain, reserving the water, and set aside.

2. Return the reserved water to the pan and bring to the boil. Add the linguine and cook for 10–12 minutes, until tender but still firm to the bite.

3. Meanwhile, heat the oil in a large frying pan over a medium–high heat. Add the onion and fry for 2–3 minutes, until translucent. Add the garlic and fry for a further minute.

4. Stir in the kale, lemon rind and chilli flakes and season to taste with salt and pepper. Cook over a medium heat for 4–5 minutes, stirring occasionally, until tender but still bright green. Add a little of the cooking water if the mixture becomes dry.

5. Drain the pasta and tip into a warmed serving dish. Add the kale mixture, tossing with the pasta to mix. Stir in the chives and Parmesan with salt and pepper to taste. Toss again and serve immediately.

HERO TIPS

Using the kale cooking water to cook the pasta not only saves time and fuel, but also gives the pasta more flavour.

SPICY AUBERGINE & CHICKPEA CASSEROLE

This hearty Middle Eastern-style vegetarian stew is packed with rich, spicy flavours. Shredded green cabbage is added towards the end of cooking so that it keeps its vibrant colour.

SERVES: 4-6   **PREP TIME: 25 MINS**   **COOK TIME: 55 MINS**

INGREDIENTS

4 tbsp olive oil

1 large onion, chopped

1 tbsp cumin seeds, crushed

½ tsp allspice berries, crushed

2 garlic cloves, thinly sliced

1 large red pepper, deseeded and cut into 2.5-cm/1-inch pieces

2 aubergines, thickly sliced and cut into segments

800 g/1 lb 12 oz canned chickpeas, drained and rinsed

400 g/14 oz canned chopped tomatoes

500 ml/17 fl oz vegetable stock

½ head of cabbage, about 280 g/10 oz, tough stems removed

salt and pepper

cooked quinoa, to serve

1. Heat the oil in a 4-litre/7-pint flameproof casserole. Add the onion, spices, ½ teaspoon salt and ¼ teaspoon pepper. Fry over a medium–high heat for 5 minutes, until the onion is soft but not coloured.

2. Add the garlic, red pepper and aubergines and fry for a further 5 minutes, until the red pepper and aubergines are beginning to soften.

3. Stir in the chickpeas, tomatoes and stock. Bring to the boil, then reduce the heat and simmer, covered, for 30 minutes.

4. Meanwhile, slice the cabbage leaves into ribbons. Add the cabbage to the casserole, cover and simmer for 10–12 minutes, until the cabbage is tender but still bright green. Taste and adjust the seasoning, adding salt and pepper if needed. Serve immediately with cooked quinoa.

CHARD & RICOTTA FILO PIE

MAKES: 9   **PREP TIME: 30 MINS**   **COOK TIME: 55 MINS**

INGREDIENTS

900 g/2 lb rainbow chard
55 g/2 oz butter
2 leeks, sliced
2 garlic cloves, thinly sliced
3 tbsp chopped mixed fresh herbs, such as thyme, marjoram and flat-leaf parsley
400 g/14 oz ricotta cheese
55 g/2 oz freshly grated Parmesan cheese
pinch of freshly grated nutmeg
2 eggs, beaten
12 large sheets filo pastry
olive oil, for brushing
55 g/2 oz pine nuts
salt and pepper

1. Chop the chard stalks into chunks. Slice the leaves into thin ribbons.

2. Heat the butter in a large frying pan over a medium heat. Add the leeks and chard stalks, cover and fry for 5–7 minutes, until soft. Add the chard leaves, garlic and herbs. Cover and gently fry until the leaves are tender. Tip the vegetables into a colander and drain.

3. Beat together the ricotta, Parmesan, nutmeg and eggs in a large bowl. Mix in the drained vegetables. Season to taste with salt and pepper.

4. Preheat the oven to 190°C/375°F/Gas Mark 5. Place one sheet of the filo pastry in an oiled 23 x 30-cm/9 x 12-inch roasting tin, trimming to fit. Brush with oil and sprinkle with a few pine nuts. Add five more sheets of pastry, lightly brushing each with oil and sprinkling with more pine nuts.

5. Pour in the filling and cover with five more sheets of filo pastry, brushing each sheet with oil and sprinkling with pine nuts. Add the final sheet and brush with oil. Using a sharp knife, cut through all the layers to make nine 7.5-cm/3-inch squares.

6. Bake in the preheated oven for 35–40 minutes, until golden and crisp. Cut into squares and serve hot or at room temperature.

KALE & BUTTER BEAN CASSEROLE

SERVES: 6

PREP TIME: 25 MINS PLUS SOAKING

COOK TIME: 2 HRS

INGREDIENTS

350 g/12 oz dried butter beans, soaked overnight

1 tbsp cumin seeds

2 tsp dried oregano

3 tbsp groundnut oil

2 onions, chopped

2 garlic cloves, thinly sliced

1–3 fresh red or green chillies, deseeded and sliced

400 g/14 oz canned chopped tomatoes

450 ml/15 fl oz vegetable stock

175 g/6 oz kale, thick stems removed, leaves shredded

5 tbsp chopped fresh coriander

juice of 1 lime

salt and pepper

TO GARNISH

2 avocados, peeled, stoned and diced

1 small red onion, halved and thinly sliced

1. Drain the beans, put them into a large saucepan and cover with water. Boil rapidly for 15 minutes, then reduce the heat and simmer for 30–45 minutes, until tender but not disintegrating. Drain and set aside.

2. Put the cumin seeds into a small dry frying pan over a medium heat and fry until fragrant. Add the oregano and fry for a few seconds, then immediately remove from the pan. Lightly crush the mixture in a mortar with a pestle.

3. Heat the oil in a large flameproof casserole over a medium heat. Add the onions and the spice and herb mixture. Fry for 5 minutes, until the onions are translucent. Add the garlic and chillies and fry for a further 2 minutes.

4. Stir in the tomatoes, beans and stock. Season to taste with salt and pepper and bring to the boil. Reduce the heat, cover and simmer for 30 minutes, stirring occasionally.

5. Increase the heat and stir in the kale. Simmer, uncovered, for 7 minutes, or until tender but still brightly coloured. Stir in the coriander and lime juice.

6. Ladle into soup plates and garnish with the avocado and red onion. Serve immediately.

GREENS, PEA & BEAN BURGERS

A mixture of peppery greens adds colour and nutrients to these mouth-watering veggie burgers. They are light yet very flavourful – even meat-eaters will gobble them up.

MAKES: 8

PREP TIME: 30 MINS PLUS STANDING

COOK TIME: 25 MINS

INGREDIENTS

115 g/4 oz peppery salad leaves, such as rocket, mustard greens, pak choi (green part only) or a mixture, thick stems removed

60 g/2¼ oz cooked peas, mashed

400 g/14 oz canned butter beans, drained, rinsed and mashed

1 tbsp grated onion

1½ tbsp chopped fresh mint

¼ tsp salt

pinch of pepper

1 egg, beaten

40 g/1½ oz stale breadcrumbs

3 tbsp vegetable oil

TO SERVE

4 oval pittas, halved crossways

cherry tomatoes, halved

mayonnaise

1. Roughly slice the salad leaves. Steam for 3 minutes, then drain and rinse under cold running water, squeezing out as much liquid as possible.

2. Combine the cooked greens with the peas, beans, onion, mint, salt, pepper and egg. Mix thoroughly with a fork. Stir in the breadcrumbs, mixing well. Leave to stand at room temperature for 30 minutes.

3. Divide the mixture into eight 1 cm/½ inch thick patties, each 6 cm/2½ inches in diameter, firming the edges well.

4. Heat the oil in a non-stick frying pan over a medium–high heat. Working in batches, add the patties and fry for 2½–3 minutes on each side, turning carefully, until golden and crisp. Meanwhile, preheat the grill to medium.

5. Toast the pitta halves under the preheated grill. Stuff each half with a bean patty, cherry tomato halves and a dollop of mayonnaise. Serve immediately.

KALE & RICOTTA CANNELLONI

SERVES: 4　　　　**PREP TIME: 45 MINS**　　　　**COOK TIME: 1 HR 20 MINS**

INGREDIENTS

350 g/12 oz kale, thick stems removed

250 g/9 oz ricotta cheese

finely grated rind of 1 lemon

1 tsp fresh thyme leaves

¼ tsp freshly grated nutmeg

40 g/1½ oz freshly grated Parmesan cheese

small handful of fresh basil leaves, torn, plus extra leaves to garnish

12 dried no pre-cook cannelloni tubes

salt and pepper

SAUCE

800 g/1 lb 12 oz canned chopped tomatoes

2 onions, quartered

55 g/2 oz butter

225 ml/8 fl oz chicken stock or vegetable stock

salt and pepper

1. To make the sauce, put the tomatoes, onions and butter in a saucepan over a medium heat. Simmer, uncovered, for 45 minutes, stirring occasionally. Strain to remove the onion, then pour back into the pan. Stir in the stock, season to taste with salt and pepper, then set aside and keep warm.

2. Meanwhile, stack the kale leaves and slice into ribbons. Steam for 5 minutes, until just tender. Drain and rinse under cold running water, squeezing out as much liquid as possible.

3. Mix the kale with the ricotta, lemon rind, thyme and nutmeg. Add half the Parmesan and the torn basil and season to taste with salt and pepper. Stuff the mixture into the cannelloni tubes, packing it in well. Preheat the oven to 180°C/350°F/Gas Mark 4.

4. Spoon half the sauce over the base of an ovenproof dish large enough to take the cannelloni tubes in a single layer. Arrange the cannelloni tubes on top and spoon over the remaining sauce. Scatter with the remaining Parmesan.

5. Cover with foil and bake in the preheated oven for 25–35 minutes, until cooked through. Garnish with basil leaves and serve immediately.

PREPARE FOR SUCCESS!

To serve greens at their best with maximum flavour and nutrients, it's well worth learning a few tricks of the trade.

Cabbage

Trim the base and separate the outer leaves. Cut out the tough stalk by slicing either side of it up into the leaf. For wedges, quarter the cabbage lengthways leaving the central core attached so the leaves don't separate. For shredded cabbage, cut out the core and slice the quarters crossways into ribbons.

Don't waste the core – it is flavoursome and crunchy. Slice it thinly and add to salads or serve as a crudité with good mayonnaise or a mustard vinaigrette.

Chard

To separate the stalks from the leaves, lay the leaf flat and slice either side of the stalk up into the leaf. Slice or dice the stalks according to the recipe. Slice the leaves into broad ribbons. Remember that they dramatically reduce in bulk when cooked.

Salad greens

Dunk leaves in cold water, then drain well and dry in a salad spinner. Spread out between layers of kitchen paper to blot up remaining moisture. Salad leaves should be perfectly dry otherwise the dressing won't cling to the leaves. To avoid bruising, tear salad greens rather than cutting them with a knife.

Broccoli

Cut calabrese-style broccoli into florets leaving about 2.5 cm/1 inch of stem attached. If the florets are large, slice them lengthways into two or three even-sized pieces so they all take the same amount of time to cook. Remember that the central stem is as tasty as the florets. Peel it and slice crossways into thin discs. Cook with the florets or stir-fry separately.

To prepare sprouting broccoli, strip the larger lower leaves from the main stem. If the stem seems tough, pull the end of the stem towards the tip until it snaps, then discard the end. Cut off the flower heads leaving about 8 cm/3¼ inches of the stem and surrounding tender leaves attached. Halve the stem lengthways if it is thick.

Kale and collard greens

To remove tough stalks, stack a few leaves on top of each other, aligning the central stalks. Fold the stack in half along the stalks.

Using a long, sharp knife, remove the stalks with a single stroke of the knife. Alternatively, hold a folded leaf in one hand, grasp the stalk with the other and strip it away.

Pak choi

To prepare pak choi, cut off the base and pull the densely packed leaves apart. Wash in several changes of water to remove any grit. The fleshy base takes longer to cook so if you are using pak choi in a stir-fry, cook the base first and add the leaves towards the end. However, tender baby pak choi can be cooked whole.

Brussels sprouts

Remove any damaged or discoloured outer leaves. Trim the base but not right up to the leaves, otherwise they'll fall off during cooking. There is no need to make the traditional cross-cut in the base – doing so allows water to penetrate further into the sprouts, making them soggy.

ROAST CHICKEN WITH WATERCRESS BUTTER

SERVES: 4 **PREP TIME: 30 MINS** **COOK TIME: 1 HR 50 MINS PLUS RESTING**

INGREDIENTS

85 g/3 oz watercress, leaves picked from the stems

100 g/3½ oz unsalted butter, at room temperature

finely grated rind and juice of 1 small orange

2 tbsp finely chopped shallot

½ tsp black peppercorns, crushed

a large pinch of sea salt

1 chicken, weighing 1.5 kg/3 lb 5 oz

400 ml/14 fl oz chicken stock

plain flour, for sprinkling

salt and pepper

1. Preheat the oven to 200°C/400°F/Gas Mark 6.

2. Chop the watercress and mix with the butter, orange rind, shallot, peppercorns and sea salt.

3. Loosen the chicken skin by pushing your fingers underneath. Insert the watercress butter under the skin, smoothing it to the shape of the bird.

4. Place the chicken breast-side down in a roasting tin. Add 6–8 tablespoons of the stock, then roast in the preheated oven for 20 minutes.

5. Turn the chicken over and reduce the oven temperature to 180°C/350°F/Gas Mark 4. Roast for a further 1 hour 15 minutes, basting occasionally, until the juices run clear when a skewer is inserted into the thickest part of the meat. Transfer the chicken to a warmed serving platter and leave to rest for 10 minutes.

6. Pour away most of the fat from the tin. Sprinkle the juices with a little flour and stir over a medium heat, scraping up the sediment from the base of the tin. Stir in the orange juice, the remaining stock and any juices that have flowed from the chicken. Bring to the boil, stirring. Check the seasoning, adding salt and pepper to taste. Strain the gravy into a jug and serve immediately with the chicken.

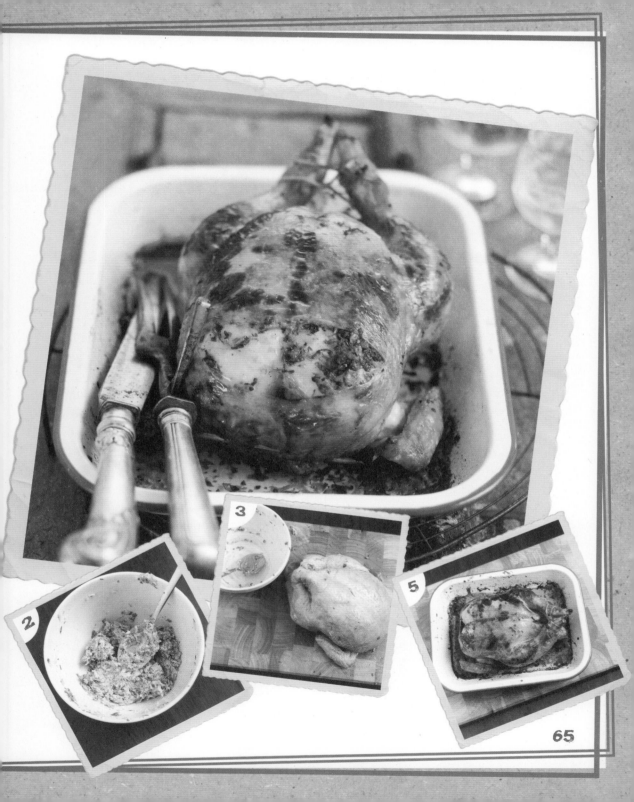

2

3

5

RED CABBAGE, TURKEY & QUINOA PILAF

Red cabbage comes into its own here, adding rich colour to this magnificent dish. Cranberries and Brazil nuts add flavour and crunch, while quinoa provides a moist and fluffy base.

SERVES: 4-6   **PREP TIME: 30 MINS**   **COOK TIME: 55 MINS**

INGREDIENTS

90 g/3¼ oz white quinoa

90 g/3¼ oz red quinoa

4 tbsp vegetable oil

1 large red onion, halved and sliced

1 tsp cumin seeds, crushed

10-cm/4-inch cinnamon stick, broken

½ head of red cabbage, core removed, leaves sliced into ribbons

250–350ml/9–12 fl oz chicken stock or vegetable stock

350 g/12 oz cooked turkey, cut into bite-sized pieces

2 carrots, shaved into ribbons

85 g/3 oz dried cranberries

85 g/3 oz Brazil nuts, roughly chopped

salt and pepper

small handful of fresh flat-leaf parsley leaves, to garnish

1. Combine the white quinoa and red quinoa, then place in a sieve and rinse under cold running water. Put in a saucepan with ½ teaspoon salt and enough water to cover by 15 mm/⅝ inch. Bring to the boil, cover and simmer over a very low heat for 15 minutes. Remove from the heat but leave the pan covered for 5 minutes to allow the grains to swell. Fluff up the grains with a fork and set aside.

2. Heat the oil in a large frying pan over a medium–high heat. Add the onion with the spices and ½ teaspoon salt and fry for 5 minutes, until the onion is soft but not coloured.

3. Add the cabbage, 250 ml/9 fl oz of the stock and ¼ teaspoon pepper. Cover and cook over a medium heat for 15–20 minutes, until the cabbage is just tender. Add the turkey, carrots, cranberries and Brazil nuts. Fry, uncovered, for 5 minutes, until the turkey is heated through.

4. Gently stir in the cooked quinoa. Add the remaining stock if the mixture seems dry and check the seasoning. Cook for 2 minutes to heat through. Garnish with parsley and serve immediately.

NEW POTATO PIZZA WITH SPINACH & PANCETTA

SERVES: 2

PREP TIME: 40 MINS PLUS RISING

COOK TIME: 25 MINS

INGREDIENTS

175 g/6 oz baby spinach, roughly chopped

3 tbsp olive oil, plus extra for oiling

300 g/10½ oz waxy potatoes, unpeeled, cooked and sliced

200 g/7 oz Gruyère cheese, grated

1 tbsp chopped fresh rosemary leaves

55 g/2 oz thinly sliced pancetta, cut into small pieces

salt and pepper

PIZZA BASE

125 g/4½ oz strong white flour

125 g/4½ oz plain flour

1 tsp salt

1 tsp easy-blend dried yeast

125–150 ml/4–5 fl oz lukewarm water

1. To make the pizza base, sift the dry ingredients into a bowl. Make a well in the centre, pour in the water and stir to a rough dough. Gather into a ball and knead for 10–15 minutes, until smooth. Place in an oiled bowl, turning to coat. Cover with clingfilm and leave in a warm place for 1½–2 hours, until doubled in size.

2. Preheat the oven to 240°C/475°F/Gas Mark 9. Oil a pizza tin. Blanch the spinach in a large saucepan of boiling water for 10 seconds. Drain and rinse under cold running water, squeezing out as much liquid as possible. Separate into small clumps.

3. Heat the oil in a large frying pan. Add the potatoes and fry for 3–4 minutes, turning, until lightly browned. Drain on kitchen paper.

4. Roll out the dough into a 30-cm/12-inch round. Place on the prepared tin. Sprinkle with 140 g/5 oz of the Gruyère and arrange the potato slices on top. Sprinkle with the rosemary and salt and pepper to taste. Arrange the spinach over the potatoes. Sprinkle with the remaining Gruyère and the pancetta.

5. Bake in the preheated oven for 10–15 minutes, turning the tin halfway through so the front is at the back, until bubbling. Serve immediately.

PORK-STUFFED CABBAGE LEAVES

SERVES: 4   **PREP TIME: 45 MINS**   **COOK TIME: 1 HR**

INGREDIENTS

1 tbsp olive oil

15 g/½ oz butter

400 g/14 oz canned chopped tomatoes

425 ml/15 fl oz chicken stock or vegetable stock

1 onion, grated

8 large cabbage leaves, thick stalks removed

300 g/10½ oz fresh pork mince

100 g/3½ oz cooked white rice

finely grated rind of 1 lemon

2 tsp paprika

½ tsp dill seeds or caraway seeds

1 egg, lightly beaten

salt and pepper

chopped fresh dill, to garnish

1. Heat the oil and butter in a large frying pan. Add the tomatoes, stock and all but 2 tablespoons of the grated onion. Season to taste with salt and pepper. Bring to the boil, then reduce the heat and simmer gently while you prepare the cabbage leaves.

2. Bring a large saucepan of water to the boil. Add the cabbage leaves and blanch for 2 minutes. Drain and rinse under cold running water, then pat dry.

3. Combine the pork, rice, lemon rind, paprika, dill seeds, egg and the remaining onion. Add ¾ teaspoon salt and ¼ teaspoon pepper and mix well. Divide the stuffing between the cabbage leaves. Fold over the base and sides of each leaf, then roll up to make a parcel.

4. Place the parcels seam-side down in the sauce. Cover and simmer over a low heat for 45 minutes, until cooked through.

5. Sprinkle with fresh dill and serve immediately.

HERO TIPS

Make sure you use a pan large enough to take the cabbage parcels in a single layer, but not so large that they can slide around and unroll.

GROW YOUR OWN

There are few greater pleasures than growing your own greens, harvesting them as and when you need to, and knowing that what you are eating is absolutely fresh. You also get to try varieties that aren't normally available in the shops.

WHAT TO GROW

There is an exciting choice in the seed catalogues, and it's easy to get carried away. It's a good idea to whittle down your options by asking yourself the following questions:

1. How much space do I have?

If room is limited, remember that a surprising number of greens can be grown in compost-filled containers. Use your imagination – builder's buckets, old sinks and dustbins are all possibilities. Window boxes are good too, especially for salad greens.

2. How much time do I have?

Don't bother with cabbages, sprouting broccoli and Brussels sprouts if you're time-poor. They take months to mature, and caterpillars love them. Go for fast and reliable croppers so you can enjoy the fruits of your labours within a few weeks.

3. What do I like to eat?

It's pointless growing spinach or Brussels sprouts if you or your family dislike them. However, if you enjoy eating salads, growing your own lettuce could save you a fortune.

THE PICK OF THE CROP
Salad greens

Salad greens are speedy growers and you can experiment with interesting varieties rarely seen in the shops.

Rocket is a must. Flavour-wise it beats shop-bought rocket, it's really easy to grow and will usually re-seed itself, giving you a year-round supply of tasty, peppery leaves.

There is a huge choice of lettuce. It's a good idea to experiment with a packet of mixed seeds so that you can see which varieties grow best in your soil. The beauty of lettuce is that you can harvest it at any stage, even as fledgling seedlings. Use the thinnings to scatter over salads or to garnish other dishes. The leaves of non-hearting lettuces can be cut at ground level and more will grow. Sow a little and often, and keep a vigilant eye out for snails and slugs.

Chard

One of the most rewarding greens to grow, chard is resistant to pests and diseases, comes with a choice of colourful stalks, and will last almost all year without bolting. It can be harvested whole, or as a cut-and-come-again crop – remove individual leaves as you need them and more will grow.

Perpetual spinach

Also known as spinach beet, this beginner-friendly plant is perfect for small spaces. As the name suggests, keep harvesting the leaves and more will grow. It will crop prolifically throughout the year and, with luck, the following year.

Pak choi

Shallow-rooted and ideal for containers, pak choi grows throughout the winter – a welcome sight when other greens are thin on the ground. Keep the crop going by harvesting leaves from the outside, or cutting whole heads just above ground level, and leaving them to re-sprout.

TUNA WITH PAK CHOI & SOBA NOODLES

SERVES: 2   **PREP TIME: 25 MINS**   **COOK TIME: 20 MINS**

INGREDIENTS

400 g/14 oz pak choi

115 g/4 oz soba noodles

2 tuna steaks, about 175 g/6 oz each and 15 mm/⅝ inch thick

2 tbsp groundnut oil, plus extra for brushing

2 slices fresh ginger, cut into matchsticks

½–1 fresh red chilli, deseeded and thinly sliced

4 spring onions, some green included, thickly sliced diagonally

140 g/5 oz frozen soya beans, thawed

2 tbsp chicken stock, vegetable stock or water

squeeze of lime juice

3 tbsp chopped fresh coriander

sea salt and pepper

1. Slice the pak choi stems into bite-sized pieces. Slice the leaves into broad ribbons.

2. Bring a large saucepan of lightly salted water to the boil. Add the noodles, bring back to the boil and cook for 5–6 minutes, until just tender. Drain, reserving the cooking water. Rinse well and set aside. Return the reserved water to the pan and keep warm over a low heat.

3. Meanwhile, cut the tuna steaks into thirds. Brush with oil and season with sea salt and pepper. Heat a ridged griddle pan over a high heat. Add the tuna and fry for 2–2½ minutes on each side. Transfer to a plate and set aside in a warm place.

4. Heat a wok over a medium–high heat. Add the 2 tablespoons oil and sizzle the ginger, chilli and spring onions for a few seconds.

5. Add the pak choi stalks, soya beans and stock and stir-fry for 3 minutes. Add the pak choi leaves and stir-fry for a further minute. Add the lime juice and coriander, then season to taste with sea salt and pepper.

6. Reheat the noodles in the cooking water, then drain. Divide the noodles between two plates, add the vegetables and arrange the tuna on top. Serve immediately.

74

2

3

5

RADICCHIO & PRAWN RISOTTO

SERVES: 3-4   **PREP TIME: 15 MINS**   **COOK TIME: 35 MINS PLUS RESTING**

INGREDIENTS

½ head of radicchio, about 150 g/5½ oz

4 tbsp olive oil

55 g/2 oz butter

2 shallots, finely chopped

375 g/13 oz risotto rice

125 ml/4 fl oz white wine

750 ml/1¼ pints hot chicken stock

2 tbsp lemon juice, plus extra to taste

40 g/1½ oz freshly grated Parmesan cheese

225 g/8 oz raw tiger prawns, peeled and deveined

salt and pepper

fresh basil leaves, to garnish

1. Remove the thick stems from the radicchio and slice the leaves crossways into ribbons.

2. Heat half the oil with half the butter in a large frying pan over a medium heat. Add the shallots and fry for 5 minutes, until soft but not coloured. Add the rice, stirring to coat the grains. Pour in the wine and stir until absorbed.

3. Add the stock, a ladleful at a time, stirring until each addition is absorbed before adding the next, until the rice is tender but still firm to the bite. When almost all the stock has been absorbed, stir in all but a handful of the radicchio, the lemon juice, Parmesan and the remaining butter. Season to taste with salt and pepper, then remove from the heat, cover and leave to rest for 5 minutes.

4. Meanwhile, heat the remaining oil in a frying pan over a medium–high heat. Add the prawns and fry for 4–5 minutes, until pink. Season to taste with salt, pepper and lemon juice.

5. Top the risotto with the prawns and the remaining radicchio leaves. Garnish with basil leaves and serve immediately.

A BIT ON THE SIDE

ROASTED KALE CRISPS

Kale's meaty flavour becomes wonderfully intense when the leaves are roasted. Torn into bite-sized pieces, they make crispy morsels that are perfect served with drinks or sprinkled over soup.

SERVES: 4　　　**PREP TIME: 15 MINS**　　　**COOK TIME: 15 MINS**

INGREDIENTS
250 g/9 oz kale
2 tbsp olive oil
2 pinches of sugar
2 pinches of sea salt
2 tbsp toasted flaked almonds, to garnish

1. Preheat the oven to 150°C/300°F/Gas Mark 2. Remove the thick stems and central rib from the kale (leaving about 125 g/4½ oz trimmed leaves). Rinse and dry very thoroughly with kitchen paper. Tear into bite-sized pieces and place in a bowl with the oil and sugar, then toss well.

2. Spread about half the leaves in a single layer in a large roasting tin, spaced well apart. Sprinkle with a pinch of sea salt and roast on the bottom rack of the preheated oven for 4 minutes.

3. Stir the leaves, then turn the tray so the back is at the front. Roast for a further 1–2 minutes, until the leaves are crisp and very slightly browned at the edges. Repeat with the remaining leaves and sea salt. Sprinkle the kale crisps with the flaked almonds and serve immediately.

HERO TIPS

It's important to put the roasting tin on the bottom rack of the oven where the heat is gentler. The leaves can easily burn, so check them often.

ROASTED BROCCOLI WITH PINE NUTS & PARMESAN

SERVES: 4　　　**PREP TIME: 20 MINS**　　　**COOK TIME: 25 MINS**

INGREDIENTS

800 g/1 lb 12 oz broccoli, in one piece
6 tbsp olive oil
1 tsp sea salt
¼ tsp pepper
4 tbsp toasted pine nuts
grated rind of ½ lemon
25 g/1 oz Parmesan cheese shavings
lemon wedges, to garnish

1. Preheat the oven to 230°C/450°F/Gas Mark 8. Cut off the broccoli crown where it meets the stalk. Remove the outer peel from the stalk. Slice the stalk crossways into 8-cm/3¼-inch pieces, then quarter each slice lengthways. Cut the crown into 4 cm/1½ inch wide wedges.

2. Put the broccoli wedges and stalks in a bowl. Sprinkle with the oil, sea salt and pepper, gently tossing to coat. Spread out in a large roasting tin. Cover tightly with foil and roast on the bottom rack of the preheated oven for 10 minutes.

3. Remove the foil, then roast for a further 5–8 minutes, until just starting to brown. Turn the stalks and wedges over, and roast for a further 3–5 minutes, until tender.

4. Tip into a shallow, warmed serving dish, together with any cooking juices. Sprinkle with the pine nuts and lemon rind, tossing to mix. Scatter the Parmesan shavings over the top.

5. Garnish with lemon wedges and serve hot, warm or at room temperature.

STIR-FRIED BRUSSELS SPROUTS WITH ALMONDS

SERVES: 4   **PREP TIME: 20 MINS**   **COOK TIME: 15 MINS**

INGREDIENTS

450 g/1 lb Brussels sprouts, tough outer leaves and stalks removed

2 tbsp groundnut oil

1 tbsp toasted sesame oil

1 shallot, finely chopped

3-cm/1¼-inch piece fresh ginger, finely chopped

1 garlic clove, thinly sliced

3–4 tbsp chicken stock or vegetable stock

juice of ½ lime

3 tbsp unskinned almonds, halved lengthways

4 tbsp chopped fresh coriander

salt and pepper

lime wedges, to garnish

1. Bring a large saucepan of water to the boil. Add the Brussels sprouts and blanch for 3 minutes. Drain and rinse under cold running water, then pat dry with kitchen paper. Slice lengthways into quarters.

2. Heat a wok or large frying pan over a medium–high heat. Add the groundnut oil and sesame oil. Add the shallot, ginger and garlic and stir-fry for 1–2 minutes, or until the garlic is just starting to colour.

3. Add the sprouts, stock and lime juice. Season to taste with salt and pepper, then stir-fry for 2–3 minutes, until the sprouts are beginning to soften. Stir in the almonds and stir-fry for 1–2 minutes, or until the sprouts are tender but still bright green.

4. Stir in the coriander, garnish with lime wedges and serve immediately.

HERO TIPS

Take care not to overcook the Brussels sprouts in step 1, otherwise they will absorb too much water and become soggy.

SPICY PAK CHOI WITH SESAME SAUCE

Pak choi, also known as bok choy, is a member of the cabbage family. Popular in Asian cooking, here it is stir-fried with chilli and garlic and drizzled with a tasty sesame sauce.

SERVES: 4   **PREP TIME: 20 MINS**   **COOK TIME: 10 MINS**

INGREDIENTS

5 small pak choi

2 tsp groundnut or vegetable oil

1 fresh red chilli, deseeded and thinly sliced

1 garlic clove, thinly sliced

100 ml/3½ fl oz vegetable stock

SAUCE

25 g/1 oz sesame seeds

2 tbsp dark soy sauce

2 tsp soft light brown sugar

1 garlic clove, crushed

3 tbsp sesame oil

1. For the sesame sauce, toast the sesame seeds in a dry frying pan over a medium heat, stirring until lightly browned. Remove from the heat and cool slightly. Transfer to a mortar. Add the soy sauce, sugar and crushed garlic and pound to a coarse paste with a pestle. Stir in the sesame oil.

2. Quarter the pak choi lengthways and set aside.

3. Heat the groundnut oil in a wok or large frying pan. Add the chilli and sliced garlic and stir-fry for 20–30 seconds. Add the pak choi and stir-fry for 5 minutes, adding the stock a little at a time to prevent sticking.

4. Transfer the pak choi to a warmed serving dish, drizzle over the sesame sauce and serve immediately.

HERO TIPS

When selecting your pak choi for this recipe, choose small ones with perky leaves and unblemished stems.

BROCCOLI WITH CAPER BUTTER SAUCE

SERVES: 4   **PREP TIME: 15 MINS**   **COOK TIME: 20 MINS**

INGREDIENTS

700 g/1 lb 9 oz purple
sprouting broccoli

3 tbsp extra virgin olive oil

3 shallots, thinly sliced

2 large garlic cloves,
thinly sliced

pinch of dried red chilli flakes

3 tbsp toasted pine nuts

55 g/2 oz butter

2 tbsp capers, drained

4 tbsp snipped fresh chives

25 g/1 oz Parmesan
cheese shavings

salt and pepper

cooked pasta, to serve

1. Cut off the broccoli florets and slice lengthways if thick. Slice the leaves and stems into 2-cm/ ¾-inch pieces. Steam over a saucepan of boiling water for 2 minutes, until barely soft. Remove from the heat and reserve the cooking water.

2. Heat the oil in a large frying pan over a low–medium heat. Add the shallots and fry for 5 minutes. Add the garlic and fry for 2–3 minutes, until just starting to colour.

3. Increase the heat to medium and add the broccoli. Add the chilli flakes and season to taste with salt and pepper. Add 3–4 tablespoons of the reserved broccoli cooking water. Cook, stirring, for 4–6 minutes, until the broccoli is just tender and still bright green.

4. Stir in the pine nuts and check the seasoning, adding salt and pepper to taste. Tip into a serving dish and keep warm.

5. Heat a heavy-based frying pan. When it is very hot, add the butter and sizzle until golden. Remove from the heat and stir in the capers and half the chives.

6. Pour the sauce over the broccoli. Sprinkle with the Parmesan shavings and the remaining chives. Serve immediately with pasta.

WHAT'S COOKING?

The rule of thumb when cooking greens is a short cooking time for crispness and colour, or long, slow cooking to bring out sweetness. If you go for the short method, remember that greens continue to cook after they have been removed from the heat.

ROASTING

Roasting is an excellent way to cook broccoli florets, or even bite-sized pieces of kale and chard. The dry heat of the oven caramelizes their natural sugars, resulting in full-on meaty flavours. Roast at a high temperature and don't overcrowd the pan.

BOILING

There are two schools of thought about boiling: one is to use a minimum amount of water so there is less liquid for vitamins to leach into; the other is to use a large volume of ready-boiling water, the advantage being speed and therefore better colour and texture. Regardless of method, it's a good idea to boil greens uncovered, otherwise acids in the steam will gather under the lid and drip onto the leaves, changing the colour to a drab olive green. To prevent red cabbage from turning blue, add a little lemon juice or vinegar to the cooking water. If you are boiling spinach, there is no need to add extra water – there will be enough left on the leaves from washing and they will eventually release their own moisture.

STEAMING

Steaming is ideal for porous greens, such as broccoli, spinach, Brussels sprouts and some types of cabbage. The vegetables are not in direct contact with the liquid so they don't become waterlogged. They retain more flavour this way and keep their vibrant colours.

FRYING

Gentle shallow-frying is a great way of wilting tender greens, such as baby spinach, young chard or rocket, before adding them to dishes like pasta or risotto. Larger, sturdier greens, such as cabbage or kale, usually need blanching in boiling water to soften them before frying or stir-frying. Stir-frying in very hot oil is easy, speedy and ideal for leafy greens, especially pak choi and Chinese cabbage. The stalks take longer to cook so slice them thinly and fry them first before adding the leaves. If you are adding greens to a mixed stir-fry, add the stalks along with other vegetables, such as carrots and onion. Stir in the leaves at the end.

BRAISING

Braising is a gentle way of cooking sturdy greens, such as kale, cabbage and collard greens. Soften the greens first by gently frying them with onion and other seasonings, then finish cooking in a covered dish with just enough water or stock to produce steam while cooking. The leaves produce their own juices, resulting in a mouth-watering dish of tender, flavour-packed greens.

BRAISED PEAS WITH LETTUCE & TARRAGON

SERVES: 4　　　**PREP TIME: 10 MINS**　　　**COOK TIME: 15 MINS**

INGREDIENTS

15 g/½ oz butter
1 tbsp olive oil
1 leek, thinly sliced
2 tsp plain flour
250 ml/9 fl oz vegetable stock
375 g/13 oz fresh or
frozen peas
2 large Little Gem
lettuces, sliced
3 tbsp chopped fresh tarragon
1 tbsp lemon juice
salt and pepper

1. Heat the butter and oil in a large saucepan. Add the leek, cover and cook over a low heat for 5 minutes, until soft. Stir in the flour, then gradually stir in the stock.

2. Add the peas, increase the heat, cover and simmer for 4 minutes. Add the lettuce without stirring it in, cover and simmer for a further 2 minutes, until the vegetables are tender.

3. Stir in the lettuce, tarragon and lemon juice. Season to taste with salt and pepper and serve immediately.

HERO TIPS

To vary the flavour, replace the tarragon with mint, or the Little Gem lettuces with chicory.

BRAZILIAN GREENS WITH BLACK BEANS & ORANGES

Kale plays the starring role in this lively Brazilian-style dish. The emerald-green leaves look stunning with black beans and orange, and kale's full-bodied flavour is a good match for chilli, garlic and coriander.

SERVES: 4   **PREP TIME: 25 MINS**   **COOK TIME: 25 MINS**

INGREDIENTS

1 large orange

3 tbsp olive oil, plus extra for drizzling

1 small onion, finely chopped

1 garlic clove, finely chopped

1 fresh green chilli, deseeded and finely chopped

600 g/1 lb 5 oz kale, thick stems removed and leaves sliced crossways

6–8 tbsp vegetable stock or chicken stock

400 g/14 oz canned black beans, drained and rinsed

6 tbsp chopped fresh coriander

salt and pepper

1. Using a sharp knife, cut a slice from the top and bottom of the orange. Remove the peel and white pith by cutting downwards, following the shape of the fruit as closely as possible. Working over a bowl, cut between the flesh and membrane of each segment and ease out the flesh. Slice each segment in half. Squeeze the membrane over the bowl to extract the juice.

2. Heat the oil in a large frying pan over a medium heat. Add the onion and fry for 5 minutes, until soft. Add the garlic and chilli, and fry for a further 2 minutes.

3. Gradually stir in the kale. Add a splash of stock, then cover and cook for 5–6 minutes, or until just wilted. Add more stock if the leaves start to look dry. Stir in the orange juice and any remaining stock. Season to taste with salt and pepper, then cover and cook for 5 minutes, until tender.

4. Stir in the beans and the orange segments. Simmer, uncovered, for a few minutes to heat through. Stir in the coriander, drizzle with a little oil and serve immediately.

STEAMED GREENS WITH LEMON & CORIANDER

This simple dish of lightly steamed crisp cabbage and velvety baby spinach is brought to life with a citrusy hit of lemon, aromatic fresh coriander and biting black pepper.

SERVES: 4   **PREP TIME: 15 MINS**   **COOK TIME: 10 MINS**

INGREDIENTS

1 head of pointed spring cabbage, weighing about 450 g/1 lb, tough outer leaves discarded

200 g/7 oz baby spinach

large knob of unsalted butter

finely grated rind of ½ lemon

4 tbsp chopped fresh coriander

sea salt and pepper

1. Cut the cabbage in quarters lengthways and cut out the tough stalk. Slice the quarters crossways into 2-cm/¾-inch ribbons. Steam for 3 minutes, until starting to soften.

2. Arrange the spinach on top of the cabbage, and steam for a further 3 minutes. Drain in a colander to remove any excess liquid.

3. Tip the cabbage and spinach into a warmed serving dish. Stir in the butter, lemon rind and coriander, mixing well.

4. Sprinkle with sea salt and pepper and serve immediately.

BROCCOLI WITH ROASTED SQUASH SAUCE

SERVES: 4   **PREP TIME: 30 MINS**   **COOK TIME: 50 MINS**

INGREDIENTS

600 g/1 lb 5 oz kabocha squash

1 small onion, halved lengthways

1 large garlic clove, unpeeled

oil, for brushing

1½ tbsp tahini

2 tsp soy sauce

squeeze of lemon juice

500 g/1 lb 2 oz purple sprouting broccoli, tough tips discarded

knob of butter

salt and pepper

1. Preheat the oven to 200°C/400°F/Gas Mark 6. Cut the squash into wedges and remove the seeds, but do not peel.

2. Place the squash in a roasting tin and tightly cover with foil. Roast in the preheated oven for 35–40 minutes, until tender.

3. Meanwhile, put the onion and garlic into a separate small roasting tin and brush with oil. Roast, uncovered, for 20 minutes, or until the onion is just coloured.

4. Peel the squash and garlic, then put the flesh into a food processor with the onion and process to a thick purée. Scrape the purée into a saucepan. Whisk in the tahini, soy sauce and lemon juice and season to taste with salt and pepper.

5. Cut off the broccoli florets and thickly slice the stems. Steam the broccoli stems and florets for 5–7 minutes, until tender but still bright green. Reserve the cooking water. Transfer the broccoli to a warmed serving dish and keep warm.

6. Use some of the broccoli cooking water to thin the squash sauce to a thick pouring consistency. Reheat over a low heat, then stir in the butter and season to taste with salt and pepper. Pour the sauce over the broccoli and serve immediately.

BRUSSELS SPROUT & RED CABBAGE SLAW

SERVES: 4

PREP TIME: 20 MINS PLUS STANDING

COOK TIME: 5 MINS PLUS COOLING

INGREDIENTS

250 g/9 oz Brussels sprouts, tough outer leaves and stalks removed

¼ head of red cabbage, weighing about 225 g/8 oz

½ tsp salt

50 g/1¾ oz pecan nuts

50 g/1¾ oz dried cranberries

6 spring onions, some green included, sliced diagonally

25 g/1 oz fresh flat-leaf parsley leaves

55 g/2 oz salad cress or radish sprouts

DRESSING

2 tsp clear honey

1½ tsp lemon juice

¼ tsp Dijon mustard

4 tbsp cold-pressed rapeseed oil or walnut oil

1. Cut the Brussels sprouts into quarters, discard the cores and slice the leaves crossways into thin shreds.

2. Remove the outer leaves and core of the red cabbage. Slice lengthways into three segments, then slice the segments crossways into thin shreds.

3. Put the sprouts and cabbage in a serving bowl and sprinkle with the salt. Toss with your hands, then set aside for 30 minutes to soften slightly.

4. Meanwhile, preheat the oven to 150°C/300°F/Gas Mark 2. Put the pecans on a small baking tray and toast in the preheated oven for 4–5 minutes. Leave to cool, then slice in half.

5. Add the pecans, cranberries, spring onions and parsley to the Brussels sprouts and cabbage, gently tossing to mix.

6. To make the dressing, whisk together all the ingredients in a small bowl or jug. Pour over the salad and gently toss. Scatter the cress over the top. Leave to stand at room temperature for 30 minutes before serving to allow the flavours to develop.

SALAD OF MIXED GREENS & HERBS

This simple salad relies on contrasting colours and flavours. Deep-green watercress, yellow-green frisée and ruby-red mustard leaves are a lovely combination with tiny pak choi leaves and soft leafy herbs.

SERVES: 4   **PREP TIME: 20 MINS**   **COOK TIME: NONE**

INGREDIENTS

8 spring onions

55 g/2 oz watercress or rocket

55 g/2 oz frisée

25 g/1 oz red mustard leaves, torn into bite-sized pieces

small handful of baby pak choi or baby kale leaves

small handful of fresh soft-leaf herbs, such as basil, mint, coriander and flat-leaf parsley

large pinch of sea salt

3–4 tbsp hazelnut oil

1 tbsp rice vinegar or white wine vinegar

55 g/2 oz toasted hazelnuts, roughly chopped

1. Trim the spring onions, keeping some of the green. Slice lengthways into 2.5-cm/1-inch shreds.

2. Put the watercress, frisée, red mustard leaves, pak choi, herbs and spring onions in a large salad bowl. Sprinkle with the sea salt. Toss gently with your hands to distribute the salt.

3. Pour in enough of the oil to barely coat the leaves and gently toss. Add the vinegar and toss again.

4. Scatter the hazelnuts over the top and serve immediately.

FRISÉE SALAD WITH WALNUT OIL DRESSING

SERVES: 4   **PREP TIME: 10 MINS**   **COOK TIME: 5 MINS
PLUS COOLING**

INGREDIENTS

½ frisée lettuce, leaves
separated and torn into
bite-sized pieces

1 romaine or cos lettuce heart,
leaves separated and torn
into bite-sized pieces

DRESSING

55 g/2 oz walnut pieces,
larger pieces broken up

3 tbsp olive oil

1 tsp runny honey

1 tbsp white wine vinegar

1 tsp Dijon mustard

pepper

1. First, make the dressing. Put the walnuts in a frying pan, add 1 tablespoon of the oil and cook over a medium heat for 2–3 minutes, or until lightly toasted. Remove from the heat, drizzle over the honey and stir; the heat from the pan will be enough to caramelize the mixture slightly.

2. Add the remaining oil to the pan and stir, then leave to cool for 15 minutes so the walnuts flavour the oil. When it is cool, put the vinegar and mustard in a small bowl, season with a little pepper and beat together, then stir into the walnuts and oil.

3. Put the frisée and romaine in a salad bowl. Spoon over the dressing, toss gently and serve immediately.

HERO TIPS

It's important to dry the leaves well after washing, otherwise the dressing won't cling to them. Use a salad spinner, then spread out the leaves on kitchen paper to blot up excess moisture. After adding the dressing, toss the salad gently with your hands.

RAINBOW SALAD WITH WASABI DRESSING

A salad doesn't need to be complicated to be good. This simple but delicious salad is an interesting way to present rainbow chard with its beautifully coloured stems and contrasting leaves.

SERVES: 4   **PREP TIME: 10 MINS**   **COOK TIME: 5 MINS PLUS COOLING**

INGREDIENTS
1 tbsp sunflower oil
4 tbsp sunflower seeds
2 tbsp soy sauce
200 g/7 oz rainbow chard

DRESSING
1 tsp wasabi paste
1 tbsp mirin
juice of 1 small orange
pepper

1. Heat the oil in a lidded frying pan over a medium heat. Add the sunflower seeds, cover with the lid and fry for 2–3 minutes, shaking the pan so they don't stick, until you hear them begin to pop. Remove the pan from the heat, add the soy sauce, cover with the lid again and leave to cool.

2. To make the dressing, put the wasabi paste, mirin, orange juice and a little pepper in a clean jam jar, screw on the lid and shake well.

3. Chop the chard stems into chunks and slice the leaves into ribbons. Put in a salad bowl, drizzle over the dressing and toss gently. Sprinkle over the toasted sunflower seeds and serve immediately.

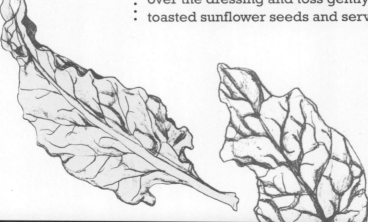

GREEN JUICES

LETTUCE & KIWI QUENCHER

Jewel-like kiwi fruits and juicy green grapes are blended with naturally sweet pear in this thirst-busting drink. Lettuce is perfect to include in a juice because it is about 90 per cent water.

SERVES: 1   **PREP TIME: 10 MINS**   **COOK TIME: NONE**

INGREDIENTS

½ romaine or cos lettuce
4 kiwi fruits, peeled
115 g/4 oz green grapes
1 large pear, halved
small handful of ice, to serve (optional)

1. Peel off a lettuce leaf and reserve for decoration.

2. Feed the kiwi fruits and grapes through a juicer, followed by the lettuce and pear.

3. Half-fill a glass with ice (if using), then pour in the juice.

4. Decorate with the reserved lettuce leaf and serve immediately.

KALE & MANGO JUICE

This pretty green-speckled drink looks mango-free, but the mango's flavour comes through even if its colour is disguised. The natural sweetness of the mango balances the strong taste of the kale.

SERVES: 1   **PREP TIME: 10 MINS**   **COOK TIME: NONE**

INGREDIENTS

1 tbsp sesame seeds
juice of ½ lime
30 g/1 oz kale, torn into pieces
1 mango, peeled, stoned and roughly chopped
225 ml/8 fl oz unsweetened soya milk
small handful of crushed ice

1. Put the sesame seeds in a blender or food processor and process until finely ground.

2. Add the lime juice, kale and mango to the blender and process again.

3. Add the soya milk and crushed ice and process until smooth.

4. Pour into a glass and serve immediately.

HERO TIPS

With its high calcium content from the sesame seeds, kale and fortified soya milk, this juice is good for your bones. Make sure that you grind the sesame seeds to a fine powder before adding the other ingredients.

SPINACH & MELON COOLER

This cleansing juice is a healthy alternative to sugar-laden commercially made drinks. The sweet and juicy melon balances out the stronger taste of the spinach, and the parsley and mint add an extra flavour zing.

SERVES: 1   **PREP TIME: 10 MINS**   **COOK TIME: NONE**

INGREDIENTS

½ Galia melon, peeled and thickly sliced

85 g/3 oz baby spinach

2 large stems of fresh flat-leaf parsley

3 large stems of fresh mint

small handful of ice (optional)

1. Feed the melon through a juicer, followed by the spinach, parsley and two stems of the mint.

2. Half-fill a glass with ice (if using), then pour in the juice.

3. Decorate with the remaining stem of mint and serve immediately.

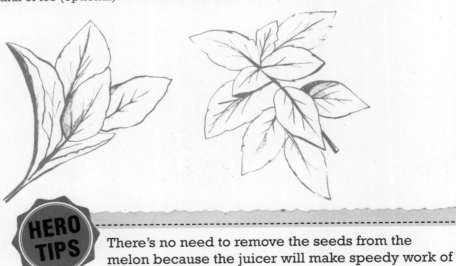

HERO TIPS

There's no need to remove the seeds from the melon because the juicer will make speedy work of separating these out.

GO FOR JUICE!

Most of us know that green vegetables are packed with health-promoting vitamins and minerals. They contain significant amounts of vitamin C and folate – a type of B vitamin needed by pregnant women and growing children – and essential minerals, such as calcium and iron. What we may not know, however, is that green vegetables are mostly water – about 75 to 90 per cent – and this makes them ideal candidates for juicing.

Drinking their juice is a convenient and instant way of getting all that goodness directly into your system. That said, vegetable juice shouldn't replace the vegetables you eat at mealtimes. Drink it as an accompaniment to a meal, or as an energy-boosting breakfast or snack.

If certain green vegetables are a challenge to eat, you'll find the juice slips down a treat. Since green vegetables contain hardly any sugar, they won't make your energy levels fluctuate in the same way as fruit and sweeter vegetables, such as carrots and beetroot, do. You can add these to balance out the flavour of the juice, but it's best to limit them to no more than one third of the total juice.

Juicing can be time-consuming and may take a while to become a habit. Advance preparation certainly helps. If you're planning on drinking juice for breakfast, it's a good idea to select the produce the night before, wash it very carefully and have the juicer set up and ready to go.

If you're new to green vegetable juice, start off with mildly flavoured romaine or iceberg lettuce, perhaps whizzed with an apple or carrot. You can then move on to spinach, chard, Chinese cabbage or crunchy pak choi. For extra depth of flavour, add a small sliver of lemon, a garlic clove or a slice of fresh ginger. If the flavour is too strong, dilute the juice with mineral water. Strongest of all are broccoli, kale and cabbage. Although they're said to be highly cleansing, their powerful flavours need taming with sweeter produce, such as apple, celery, cucumber, fennel or carrot.

Vegetable juice is highly perishable. Once exposed to light, heat and air, the nutrients are partially destroyed, so it should be drunk right away. If you have to store your juice, put it in a sealed container in the refrigerator for no more than 24 hours.

BROCCOLI & PARSLEY REVITALIZER

Wonderfully soothing and gentle, this delicate, reviving green juice is naturally sweet and refreshing, and makes a perfect alternative to a caffeine-loaded tea or coffee in the afternoon.

SERVES: 1   **PREP TIME: 10 MINS**   **COOK TIME: NONE**

INGREDIENTS

115 g/4 oz broccoli, broken into large florets

small handful of fresh flat-leaf parsley

½ fennel bulb

2 apples, halved

chilled water, to taste (optional)

small handful of ice (optional)

1. Feed the broccoli and parsley through the juicer, followed by the fennel and apples.

2. Top up the juice with chilled water to taste, if desired.

3. Half-fill a glass with ice (if using), then pour in the juice. Serve immediately.

HERO TIPS

There's no need to add water to the juice if you don't want to – it depends on how thirsty you are and how strong the juice tastes.

ROCKET, APPLE & GINSENG REFRESHER

Rocket has a peppery flavour so if you're new to green juices, then this might not be the one to start you off. Ginseng is a natural stimulant that helps to combat stress and lifts the mood.

SERVES: 1　　　**PREP TIME: 10 MINS**　　　**COOK TIME: NONE**

INGREDIENTS

1 ginseng tea bag or
1 tsp ginseng tea
150 ml/5 fl oz boiling water
1 apple, halved
40 g/1½ oz rocket

1. Put the tea bag in a cup, pour over the boiling water and leave to infuse for 4 minutes. Strain the tea into a glass.

2. Feed the apple through a juicer, followed by the rocket.

3. Stir the juice into the tea and serve warm.

HERO TIPS

This revitalizing drink can also be enjoyed cold. Simply leave to cool, then drop in some ice cubes and stir well before serving.

KALE, LETTUCE & AVOCADO JUICE

It would be easy to believe that just looking at this green drink could make you feel healthier! The good news is that it really is bursting with vitamins and minerals.

SERVES: 1   **PREP TIME: 10 MINS**   **COOK TIME: NONE**

INGREDIENTS

55 g/2 oz kale

small handful of fresh flat-leaf parsley

½ romaine or cos lettuce

3 celery sticks, halved

1 apple, halved

½ lemon

30 g/1 oz flaked almonds

½ avocado, peeled and stoned

small handful of crushed ice (optional)

1. Feed the kale through a juicer, followed by the parsley and lettuce. Finally, feed two of the celery sticks, the apple and lemon through the juicer.

2. Put the flaked almonds in a blender or food processor and process until finely ground.

3. Add the juice and avocado flesh to the almonds, and process until smooth. Add the crushed ice (if using) and blend again.

4. Pour the juice into a glass. Decorate with the remaining celery stick and serve immediately.

SPINACH, WATERCRESS & COURGETTE BOOSTER

If you like spinach or watercress soup, you'll love this juice. You don't get a huge amount of juice from these green leaves, but what you do get is concentrated with antioxidants, minerals and vitamins.

SERVES: 1　　　　**PREP TIME: 10 MINS**　　　　**COOK TIME: NONE**

INGREDIENTS
55 g/2 oz baby spinach
30 g/1 oz watercress
1 courgette, halved
2 apples, halved
1 tsp wheatgrass powder (optional)
small handful of ice (optional)

1. Feed the spinach and watercress through a juicer, followed by the courgette and apples.

2. Stir the wheatgrass powder (if using) into the juice.

3. Half-fill a glass with ice (if using), then pour in the juice. Serve immediately.

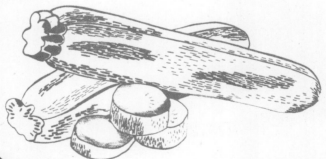

HERO TIPS

Unless you have a masticating juicer, fresh wheatgrass can be difficult to juice. The powdered wheatgrass used in this recipe is easier to use, although it doesn't contain quite as much nutrition.

SPINACH, CUCUMBER & AVOCADO JUICE

This super-smooth green juice is packed with antioxidants, vitamins and minerals. It would be a fantastic choice for breakfast, giving you an energy boost without making you feel heavy.

SERVES: 1   **PREP TIME: 10 MINS**   **COOK TIME: NONE**

INGREDIENTS

1 pear, halved
¼ cucumber, roughly chopped
40 g/1½ oz baby spinach
4 stems of fresh flat-leaf parsley
½ avocado, peeled and stoned
½ tsp spirulina powder
chilled water
1 Brazil nut, roughly chopped

1. Feed the pear and cucumber through a juicer.

2. Pour the juice into a blender or food processor, then add the spinach, parsley and avocado, and blend until smooth. Pour the juice into a glass.

3. Mix the spirulina powder with just enough chilled water to make a thick liquid, then swirl it into the juice.

4. Sprinkle over the chopped Brazil nut, then serve immediately.

HERO TIPS

Look for packs of spirulina powder in health-food shops. This fine, white powder turns a dark shade of green when mixed with water. Made from a cultivated algae, it's a great protein-booster.

Index